DIVINE INVASIONS

STUDY GUIDE

Experience God's Miracles in Your Life Today

DR. ROBERT JEFFRESS

BakerBooks
a division of Baker Publishing Group
Grand Rapids, Michigan

Published by Baker Books
a division of Baker Publishing Group
Grand Rapids, Michigan
BakerBooks.com

Printed in the United States of America

ISBN 9781540904447 (paper)
ISBN 9781493456550 (ebook)

Portions of this text have been adapted from *Divine Invasions: Experience God's Miracles in Your Life Today* (Baker, 2026).

Cover design by Peter Gloege, Look Design Studio

Published in association with Yates & Yates, www.yates2.com.

Baker Publishing Group publications use paper produced from sustainable forestry practices and post-consumer waste whenever possible.

26 27 28 29 30 31 32 7 6 5 4 3 2 1

CONTENTS

INTRODUCTION and Tips for Study Groups

Before beginning your personal or group study of *Divine Invasions: Experience God's Miracles in Your Life Today*, please take time to read these introductory comments.

If you are working through the study on your own, you may want to adapt certain sections (for example, the icebreakers) and record your responses to the questions in this study guide or, if preferred, a separate notebook. You might find it more enriching or motivating to study with a partner with whom you can share answers or insights.

If you are leading a group, you may want to ask group members to read one chapter from the *Divine Invasions* book and work through the corresponding questions in this study guide before each meeting. This isn't always easy for busy adults, so encourage group members with occasional phone calls, emails, or texts between meetings. Help group members manage their time by pointing out that they can cover a few pages each day. Also, encourage them to identify a regular time of the day or week that they can devote to the study. They, too, may write their responses to the questions in this study guide or in a separate notebook.

Each session in this study guide includes the following features:

- **Session Topic**—a brief statement summarizing the session.
- **Icebreakers**—activities to help group members get better acquainted with the session topic and/or with one another.
- **Group Discovery Questions**—questions to encourage group participation or individual discovery.
- **Personal Application Questions**—an aid to applying the knowledge gained through study to personal living. (Note: these are important questions for group members to answer for themselves, even if they do not wish to discuss their responses in the meeting.)
- **Optional Activities**—supplemental applications that will enhance the study.
- **Prayer Focus**—suggestions for turning learning into prayer.
- **Assignment**—activities or preparation to complete prior to the next session.

Here are a few tips that can help you more effectively lead small group studies:

1. *Pray for each group member during the week.* Ask the Lord to help you create an open atmosphere where everyone will feel free to share with one another.

2. *Ensure each group member has the* Divine Invasions *book and study guide.* Encourage each group member to bring his or her book and study guide, a pen or pencil, and a Bible to each session. This study is based on the New American Standard Bible (1995), but it is good to have several Bible translations on hand for purposes of comparison.
3. *Start and end on time.* This is especially important for the first meeting because it will set the pattern for the rest of the sessions.
4. *Begin each study session with prayer.* Ask the Holy Spirit to open hearts and minds and to give understanding so that truth will be applied.
5. *Involve everyone in the group discussion.* As learners, we retain some of what we hear and see, but we remember much more of what we hear, see, and do.
6. *Promote a relaxed environment.* If the group is meeting in person, arrange the chairs in a circle or semicircle. This allows eye contact among members and encourages dynamic discussion. Be relaxed in your attitude and manner, and be willing to share with the group.

CHAPTER 1

DIVINE INVASIONS

Session Topic

God is still in the miracle-working business. That's why God preserved so many stories of miracles in the Bible, along with stories of modern-day miracles such as those you'll read about in this book: to teach us that He is able to answer our prayers and intervene in our lives. Yes, God is able to supernaturally work a miracle in your life, if He chooses to do so. But even if He chooses not to, as we're going to see, He still is able to unleash His supernatural power in giving you peace so that you can endure the circumstances you're experiencing.

Icebreakers (Choose One)

1. What interested you in joining this study of *Divine Invasions*, and what do you hope to gain as a result of this study?

2. Have you studied biblical miracles before? What is your attitude toward miracles?

Group Discovery Questions

1. What comes to mind when you think of the word *miracle*?

2. Discuss some of the ways the word *miracle* is used in our society. Are most of these things actual miracles? Why or why not?

3. What did you learn in chapter 1 about the difference between essentials and nonessentials in Christian doctrine? According to the author, is our particular view of miracles essential or nonessential? Explain your answer.

4. What changed the author's mind about the reality of miracles today? Have you changed your mind about the reality of miracles from what you used to believe?

5. Consider the author's statement: "God can and does work miracles today if He so chooses; He's just eliminated the need for a middleman." Based on your reading, why does the author say that God no longer needs a "middleman" to do a miracle? Why is that significant?

6. Review the five purposes for God's miracles described in chapter 1. Briefly discuss what you learned about each of these purposes. Which one stands out most to you, and why?

7. Discuss what you learned about the four Greek terms used in the New Testament to describe miracles: *dunamis* ("mighty works"), *semeion* ("signs"), *terata* ("wonders"), and *erga* ("works"). How do these words differ? In what ways did your study of these words give you a better understanding of miracles?

Personal Application Questions

1. What is your current view on miracles? Do you think miracles happened only in the days of the Bible, or do you believe God still works miracles today? Explain your answer.

2. When you hear people talk about miracles, what emotions do you experience? In what ways would you like your perspective on miracles to be influenced by this study?

3. Have you or someone you know experienced what you consider to be a miracle? If so, describe what happened.

4. Of the four types of miracles covered in *Divine Invasions* (miracles of power, provision, protection, and healing), which one are you most interested in studying, and why?

5. Read Hebrews 13:8. In what ways can this truth about Jesus Christ influence your perspective on miracles?

6. The author says, "The Bible also includes acts of God's *miraculous providence* in the lives of His children." According to your reading, what is miraculous providence? List a few examples of God's miraculous providence in the Bible.

7. Can you think of a time when you experienced God's miraculous providence, demonstrating His sovereign control over the people and events in your life? Describe what happened.

Optional Activities

1. Divide into groups of two or more and discuss what you learned this week about how God demonstrates that He is at work in the world today. Share any experiences of God's "divine invasions" in your life or the life of someone important to you, and then close in prayer, giving God praise.

2. Ask yourself the following questions, and take note of any divine invasions you may have experienced in your life so far:
   - Can you look back and see a supernatural answer to prayer—when you prayed for something and only God could be the one who answered that prayer?
   - Can you look back and see a word of encouragement that you needed that came at just the right time?
   - Can you remember a need you had that no one or only a few people knew about that was dramatically met, and there's no other way to explain it except as the hand of God?
   - Can you recall several things that happened in your life at just the right time—events that only God could have orchestrated to happen when they did?

Prayer Focus

Thank God for being the same yesterday, today, and forever. Confess any doubts or questions you may have about God's miracles, and ask Him to give you a new sense of His power and presence in your life as you focus on our miracle-working God during this study.

Assignment

1. On a blank note card or sticky note, write the following truth: *God is still in the miracle-working business!* Place this note somewhere you will see it every day this week as a reminder of God's miraculous power. Consider how this perspective influences your daily attitudes and activities, and be prepared to share your insights with the group next week.

2. Read chapter 2 of *Divine Invasions* and work through the corresponding study.

CHAPTER 2

MIRACLES OF POWER

Session Topic

Although every miracle involves God's power, there are certain miracles that display His supernatural power in a dramatic way. When we investigate the pages of Scripture, we discover five periods of time when God's power was on full display in dramatic ways. But that doesn't mean His power has diminished in any way today. God can do anything that is in accordance with His will, including working a miracle in your life.

Icebreakers (Choose One)

1. What is your favorite miracle story in the Bible, and why?

2. Describe a time when you felt small and puny compared to God's vastness. How did you respond to that experience?

Group Discovery Questions

1. How does God use divine providence in people's lives to direct His plans for them? Give a few specific examples.

2. According to the author, the Bible records "five periods of time with God's power on full display in dramatic ways. Four of those periods are past, and one is future." Review and discuss the four past periods when miracles were prominent and God intervened actively in history. Why was it important for God to display His power and glory through miracles during those times?

3. What did you learn about the fifth period of time when the Bible says there will be great signs and wonders on earth? What will be the final great miracle, which the author calls "the miracle we're all looking forward to"?

4. Read Psalm 145:9, Matthew 5:45, Luke 6:35, and Acts 14:17. What do you learn from these passages about "common grace"? Who receives this type of miracle? In what ways does common grace differ from the special grace God shows to His children?

5. According to the author, there are two aspects of the Holy Spirit related to God's power in your life: *the indwelling of the Spirit* (Rom. 8:9) and *the filling of the Spirit* (Eph. 5:18). Discuss what you learned about both of these in your reading.

6. Consider the author's statement: "God can do anything that is in accordance with His will, including working a miracle in your life. His power is available to us today because He has promised to make it available." Read the following Scriptures and discuss what you learn about God's power: Genesis 18:14; Job 42:2; Jeremiah 32:17, 27; Zechariah 8:6; Matthew 19:26; Mark 10:27; Luke 1:37; 18:27.

7. Read Isaiah 40:28–31. What does this passage reveal about God's attributes, character, and relationship with us?

8. What are the four principles outlined in chapter 2 that discuss how believers can access God's power? Who is God's power for, and how is it accessed? What resources should we use to experience the power of God in our lives?

Personal Application Questions

1. Have you ever faced a situation in which you needed God's power in your life? Describe what happened.

2. Read Psalm 86:1–13. Which verse in this passage stands out most to you right now, and why?

3. According to the author, "Most of our experiences of God's power in our lives today fall under the category of His *miraculous providence*—subtle demonstrations of His care for us." Describe a time when God demonstrated His care for you through His miraculous providence.

4. The author quoted this Jewish prayer: "Privileged, O Lord, are we to live in this generation."[1] What are some of the benefits we enjoy today that were not available to believers in the past? In what ways would your attitudes and actions be different if you said this prayer every day?

5. Consider the author's statement: "The Scripture is clear on this point. In fact, it's repeated throughout the Old and New Testaments: *Nothing is impossible with God*. We just need to come to the omnipotent God in faith." What request do you need to bring before the Lord in faith today?

6. We learned in chapter 2 that "human prayer and divine power are mysteriously linked." Why do you think there's a relationship between our asking and God's answering?

1. Jewish prayer from the time of the Maccabees, as quoted in Os Guinness, *Carpe Diem Redeemed: Seizing the Day, Discerning the Time* (InterVarsity, 2019), 87.

7. What circumstances in your life are causing you to feel weak or powerless right now? Be specific. Reread Isaiah 40:28–31 and reflect on the author's insights about this passage: "God doesn't just possess all power; He gives power to the weak. God doesn't just possess all energy; He gives energy to the fatigued. All you need to do is 'wait for the LORD'—rest in hope, looking to God to supply your need—and He will give you strength, exchanging His power for your powerlessness." Spend some time in prayer, asking God to give you His strength.

Optional Activities

1. Divide into groups of two or more and look up the following miracles of Jesus. Which one stands out to you most, and why?
    - Two blind men receive sight: *Matthew 9:27–31*
    - A paralyzed man is healed: *Mark 2:1–12*
    - A leper is cleansed: *Luke 5:12–14*
    - A dead man is raised to life: *John 11:1–45*
    - Jesus walks on water: *Matthew 14:22–33*
    - Jesus calms a storm: *Mark 4:35–41*
    - Jesus fills nets with fish: *Luke 5:1–11*
    - Jesus turns water into wine: *John 2:1–11*
    - Jesus multiplies food: *Matthew 14:13–21*; *Mark 6:33–44*; *Luke 9:12–17*; *John 6:1–14*

2. Reflect on these four questions from the chapter and answer honestly with yes or no.
   - Are you a child of God?
   - Are you being filled daily by the Spirit of God?
   - Are you spending time in the Word of God?
   - Are you praying to access the power of God?

Confess to God any *no* answers that may be limiting your experience of His power in your life. Ask Him to help you take the next steps to answer *yes* to all these questions, so you can watch for the God of power to work miracles of power in your life when you need Him most.

Prayer Focus

Thank God for allowing you to live in this generation, with the completed Scriptures and the indwelling Holy Spirit. Bring your needs before the Lord in prayer and watch for the God of power to work miracles of power in your life when you need them most.

Assignment

1. Memorize Isaiah 40:28–29: "Do you not know? Have you not heard? The Everlasting God, the LORD, the Creator of the ends of the earth does not become weary or tired. His understanding is inscrutable. He gives strength to the weary, and to him who lacks might He increases power."

2. Read chapter 3 of *Divine Invasions* and work through the corresponding study.

CHAPTER 3

MIRACLES OF PROVISION

Session Topic

Sometimes we see God's provision in the rearview mirror—in hindsight, after the fact. And sometimes we see God's provision stretching out before us, like a straight road with signs along the way. However God chooses to invade our lives, we can rest assured that He will care for our needs.

Icebreakers (Choose One)

1. Describe a time when God met a need for you. How did that provision encourage you?

2. Ask each group member to list at least three provisions from God they are grateful for.

Group Discovery Questions

1. According to your reading, how did God give assurance to the author that He would provide for First Dallas's building program during a financially trying time? In what ways did that answered prayer encourage other believers and churches?

2. Discuss what you learned in this chapter about the three types of provision we need: food in our stomachs, clothes on our backs, and a roof over our heads. In what ways has God provided for these needs in your life?

3. Read 2 Thessalonians 3:10, Hebrews 13:5, and 1 Timothy 6:9–10. What do you learn about money from these verses? How can we fulfill our need for money while avoiding the temptation to worship money and the things it provides?

4. God is a triune being—Father, Son, and Holy Spirit—and since we are made in His image, we, too, are designed to be relational beings. What things do you see in society today that are drawing people away from building relationships? How can we avoid getting caught in the trap of becoming isolated from others so we can instead bring glory to God through our relationships?

5. Read Matthew 7:7–8. What did you learn in this chapter about the "principle of A.S.K."? Describe what you learned about prayers of *persistence* and prayers of *boldness*.

6. According to James 4:3, why might God withhold an answer to our prayers for His provision?

7. Read 2 Corinthians 9:7–9 and Philippians 4:19. When God blesses us with abundance (provision that is more than our needs), how are we to use that abundance? When we are faithful to share our abundance with others, what does that reveal about our hearts?

Personal Application Questions

1. When was the last time the Lord met a need in your life? Can you trace His fingerprints on that situation? Pause for a moment to thank God for His miraculous provision for you.

2. In what ways has God provided for your need for someone to love, a place to belong, and a roof over your head? Be specific. Thank God for His miraculous provision in your life.

3. What big thing do you want to see God provide in your life right now? Be specific.

4. Read Psalm 145:14–16. How do these promises from God give you encouragement in whatever situation you are facing?

5. If God already knows our needs, why do we need to ask Him to provide for them? What happens to our will when we pray sincerely, seeking God's will?

6. Are you grateful when God provides for your physical needs in life? What are some ways we can make sure we are recognizing that the source of our provision is God?

7. Read Psalm 34:8. When you are faced with the storms of life, in what ways does God provide you with refuge? What does it mean for you to take refuge in God?

Optional Activities

1. As a group, consider the author's statement: "The principle of generosity highlights the truth that God bestows blessings on us in proportion to the blessings we bestow on others." How can God work through you to be His hands and feet of provision for those who have needs in your church and community? Make a specific plan to use your abundance to meet someone's need this week.

2. Read Matthew 6:31–33. How can you "seek first His kingdom and His righteousness" in your life right now? When we make it a priority to live on earth as if we are living in heaven, where God's will and God's glory are the most important things in life, then God will meet our earthly needs.

Prayer Focus

Thank God for His promise to provide for you and praise Him for all the ways He has provided for your needs so far. Ask God for the big thing you want Him to provide in your life right now, knowing that He's ready and willing to care for your needs.

Assignment

1. Psalm 34:8–10 says, "O taste and see that the LORD is good; how blessed is the man who takes refuge in Him! O fear the LORD, you His saints; for to those who fear Him there is no want. The young lions do lack and suffer hunger; but they who seek the LORD shall not be in want of any good thing." Think of someone you know who would be comforted by this promise, and reach out to that person this week to share words of comfort and hope about God's provision in our lives.

2. Read chapter 4 of *Divine Invasions* and work through the corresponding study.

CHAPTER 4

MIRACLES OF PROTECTION

Session Topic

Whether because of natural disasters, accidents, criminal activity, or warfare, physical dangers are simply part and parcel of living in a fallen world. Though dangers surround us and may spring upon us suddenly, we aren't defenseless. God repeatedly encourages us to pray for His protection against every kind of danger we can imagine.

Icebreakers (Choose One)

1. Have you personally experienced miraculous protection or know someone close to you who has? If so, describe what happened.

2. Describe one of your favorite Bible stories in which God demonstrated His miraculous protection. In what ways does that Bible story encourage you in your own need for protection?

Group Discovery Questions

1. What are some of the physical dangers we face as part of living in a fallen world?

2. What are some of the spiritual dangers believers experience today? Be specific. According to Ephesians 6:10–12, what is the source of these spiritual dangers?

3. What are some of the ways Christians can be led astray, distracted, or deceived in our faith? In what ways can these spiritual dangers affect not only the individual Christian but also the local church and the whole body of Christ?

4. Consider the author's statement: "Though dangers surround us and may spring upon us suddenly, we aren't defenseless." According to your reading, what is our first line of defense when we're in a dangerous situation and need God's protection? Do most believers immediately apply this first line of defense when faced with physical or spiritual danger? Why or why not?

5. Read Psalm 22:20–21. In this psalm, David was praying for protection from the common sources of danger in his day: warfare, animal attacks, and accidents. If David were praying that prayer today, what kinds of things do you think he might include?

6. Discuss what you learned in this chapter about the three principles of protection: *direct fortification*, *angelic intervention*, and *the Spirit's direction*. How can each one give us confidence in our lives so we do not live in fear? Instead of focusing on the dangers around us, where should our focus be?

7. According to the author, "The Holy Spirit is like [a] generator. He is always present in us, but there are four conduits that activate His power in us: the Bible, prayer, the church, and obedience to God." Why is it important for believers to apply all four conduits of the Holy Spirit in our lives? What might happen if we consistently neglect one or more of them?

Personal Application Questions

1. Read Psalm 139:16. According to this verse, who is in control of how many days each of us will live? How can this truth give you comfort when you're facing a dangerous situation?

2. Have you or someone you know ever experienced a "close call" where you inexplicably avoided a serious accident or worse? If so, describe what happened, and thank the Lord for demonstrating His miraculous protection over you.

3. Has God ever protected you from giving in to a spiritual danger, such as false teaching, conflict with Christian brothers and sisters, or distractions that keep you busy with the things of the world so you won't attend to the things of the Spirit?

4. Read Proverbs 3:5. You can trust in the Lord. There's nothing to fear because our God is the Rock who provides a hedge around you, your family, and your possessions. On a scale of 1 to 10, how high is your trust meter? What do you need to do to increase it a notch or two?

5. This chapter describes four truths about God that we can bank on: *God is sovereign*, *God is awake*, *God is a shelter*, and *God is a shield*. How can each truth give you confidence in the face of danger? Which truth stands out to you most in your current situation, and why?

6. Read Romans 8:31. Ask the Lord to open your eyes to His sovereign power when the next trouble or danger crosses your path.

7. Consider the author's statement: "Courage in the face of danger is one of the great gifts of the Holy Spirit." Have you ever experienced supernatural courage from the Holy Spirit? Read 2 Timothy 1:7 to learn more about what the Holy Spirit gives us.

Optional Activities

1. Get into groups of two or more and look up the following verses: Psalm 31:8; 56:13; 66:9; 125:1; Proverbs 2:8; 3:21, 23, 25–26. Discuss what you learn from these verses about God's miraculous protection.

2. Reflect on the author's statement: "We should never expect the Holy Spirit to provide more direction in our lives if we are not following the direction He has already provided for us." In what ways have you been following the Holy Spirit's direction in your life? In what areas of your life would you like to follow the Spirit's direction more closely? Spend some time in prayer, asking God to help you "walk by the Spirit" (Gal. 5:25).

Prayer Focus

Use David's words in Psalm 139:23–24 as your prayer: "Search me, O God, and know my heart; try me and know my anxious thoughts; and see if there be any hurtful way in me, and lead me in the everlasting way."

Assignment

1. Set a time and place to kneel before your Creator every day this week to confess your sins, express gratitude for His goodness, and pour out your requests to Him, including asking for His protection over you and your loved ones. Write this appointment with God on your calendar, and be sure to keep it every day.

2. Read chapter 5 of *Divine Invasions* and work through the corresponding study.

CHAPTER 5

MIRACLES OF HEALING

Session Topic

The author wrote, "I'm skeptical of faith healers, but I firmly believe in faith healing—that our great and good God, according to His purposes, can heal us." But it's important to remember that healing is not limited to our bodies but encompasses the whole person. Everyone who places faith in Christ will be ultimately healed when we are in the physical presence of the Lord.

Icebreakers (Choose One)

1. Do you know someone who has experienced a miracle of physical healing? If so, describe what happened.

2. How do some people today attempt to seek physical and spiritual healing apart from medical doctors?

Group Discovery Questions

1. According to the author, "In the United States, physical health and wellness are big business." Discuss a few specific ways that people today participate in this booming physical health and wellness industry. Are these kinds of activities, techniques, and supplements helpful? Why or why not?

2. Consider the author's statement: "The ancient Hebrews viewed humans as whole beings. They taught that physical pain affects the spirit—what we might call mental and emotional health—and that spiritual pain affects physical health." Do you agree or disagree with this perspective? Explain your answer.

3. Read Psalm 32:3–7. What phrases did David use to describe how his sin-sick spirit affected his physical body? What was his turning point in verse 5?

4. According to Isaiah 53:5, what is the healing that Jesus provided for us on the cross? What is the disease we need to be healed from through the blood of Jesus?

5. Read Revelation 21:4. When will believers experience perfect and complete healing of all our diseases? In what way does this promise of your ultimate, eternal healing affect your perspective of physical illness here on earth?

6. This chapter explains two principles of God's providential care for your physical health: *preventive* actions and *prescriptive* actions. Discuss what you learned about each of these actions. In which areas are you doing well? In which areas do you need to improve?

7. Based on what you learned in this chapter, what are some of the causes of illness? How can either physical healing or a lack of healing be for God's glory?

Personal Application Questions

1. On a scale of 1 to 10, how afraid are you of getting older and losing your health or physical abilities?

2. Read Ecclesiastes 12:1–7 and review what you learned in your reading about Solomon's description of old age. Which of these phrases do you identify with?

3. What are some ways we try to delay the inevitable aging process that brings loss of vigor and health today? Have you been guilty of overdoing it in an attempt to stay young? What were the results of overdoing it?

4. This chapter discusses the connection between physical health and emotional health. In what ways have you experienced the effects of emotional stress on your physical body? What steps did you take (or can you take now) to alleviate that stress and care for your physical health?

5. Read Luke 2:52, then review what you learned in this chapter about how Jesus "kept increasing in . . . stature" (improved physically) by practicing good health. Which of these preventive actions do you need to pray about and work on in your life?

6. Based on what you read in this chapter, what steps do you need to take when you are ill? Why do you need to pray if you have access to medicine and doctors?

7. Reflect on the author's statement: "When it comes to praying for healing, faith is boldly asking God to do what we want and quietly trusting in Him to do what is best." Spend some time in prayer, boldly asking God to heal you or someone you know and trusting Him to do what's best.

Optional Activities

1. Break into groups of two or more and discuss how God's promise of your future ultimate healing can affect your perspective on life now. Be as specific as possible.

2. Read the description of the new heaven and earth in Revelation 21:2–4. What are you looking forward to most on that day? Who can you invite to join you in the new heaven and earth by sharing with them the gospel of salvation? Pray for these unbelievers and ask God to give you opportunities to share the gospel so they, too, can be part of this celebration.

Prayer Focus

Thank God for His promise that everyone who places faith in Christ will ultimately be healed when we are with Him in heaven. Confess any ways you have been either neglecting or overfocusing on your physical health. Boldly ask God for what you desire and quietly trust Him to do what is best in your life.

Assignment

1. Memorize Revelation 21:4: "He will wipe away every tear from their eyes; and there will no longer be any death; there will no longer be any mourning, or crying, or pain; the first things have passed away." That's a promise to cling to!

2. Read chapter 6 of *Divine Invasions* and work through the corresponding study.

CHAPTER 6

WHEN YOUR MIRACLE DOESN'T COME

Session Topic

There are any number of reasons God might not answer our prayers, including our prayers for a miracle. When your hoped-for and prayed-for miracle doesn't come, don't look for a way of escape or turn your back on the Lord for His failure to deliver what you want; instead, dive deeper into God's Word to find the grace and faith to go on.

Icebreakers (Choose One)

1. Have you or a loved one needed a miracle, but it didn't come? If so, describe what happened.

2. Think of a believer who suffered in this life and glorified God through his or her suffering. Share how that person's faith in God throughout his or her struggle inspired or encouraged you.

Group Discovery Questions

1. What are some false conclusions we can make about God when He doesn't answer our prayers?

2. Read Hebrews 11:1, 6. How does the writer to the Hebrews define *faith*? During times of suffering, why is it important for us to believe that God is who He says He is and that He can and will do what He says He will do?

3. According to the author, there are at least seven reasons God might not answer our prayers, including our prayers for a miracle. Read the following verses and discuss what is limiting God's answer in each one: Psalm 66:18; James 1:5–8; 1 John 3:22; 1 Corinthians 10:31; 1 Thessalonians 4:3; Luke 18:9–14; Ephesians 6:18.

4. Read 2 Corinthians 12:7–10. In this passage, what did the apostle Paul call the ailment he struggled with? How many times did he pray and beg God to remove that suffering? What was God's answer to his prayers? Discuss what you learned from this passage about God and about His answers to our prayers.

5. Reflect on the author's statement: "The Lord sometimes tests our faith before He answers our prayers." Read James 1:2–4. According to this passage, what is God's goal for us when He tests our faith? Why do you think unanswered prayers are sometimes necessary to achieve that goal in our lives?

6. Read 2 Corinthians 4:17–18. Why do you think the apostle Paul referred to suffering as "momentary, light affliction"? To what did he compare our earthly trials? How could that perspective help him (and us) endure suffering joyfully?

7. Discuss the author's statement: "If your miracle doesn't come, you can rest assured it doesn't mean God has forgotten about you or doesn't love you. It may mean God has a purpose for your suffering that you can't yet see. Or perhaps God may be using your suffering for something better. Your life doesn't consist of avoiding suffering but of turning your suffering into something good."

Personal Application Questions

1. When your miracle doesn't come, do you tend to respond with an attitude of self-pity or bitterness? What can you do to make joy your leading thought whenever you experience some difficulty or disappointment?

2. Reflect on the author's statement: "If we endure in our faith—being obedient to follow God in every decision we make—God sometimes replaces what could have been a miracle with an even greater miracle!" Has God ever said no to your prayer request, only to provide you with an even greater miracle? Describe what happened.

3. Read Colossians 3:2. While you are praying for your miracle, what are some specific things you can do to "set your mind on the things above"?

4. Romans 8:28 says, “We know that God causes all things to work together for good to those who love God, to those who are called according to His purpose.” What is the “good” Paul had in mind here? (Hint: He describes it in verse 29.)

5. Read 2 Corinthians 1:3–4, and then reflect on the author’s statement: “The real key to 2 Corinthians 1:3–4 is not that we find comfort in the Son, the Spirit, and the saints ourselves but that *we comfort (strengthen) others*.” In what ways has your own suffering in life equipped you to minister to others who may be experiencing something similar?

6. According to the author, “No matter how heavy the burden is that you are carrying, it is light in comparison to the joy you will experience in heaven one day.” In a journal or on a separate piece of paper, write a list of burdens you are carrying right now, and then write another list of the joys you will experience in heaven. How does this exercise affect your perspective on your circumstances?

7. Read Hebrews 11. How do these examples of faithful men and women demonstrate the truth that miracles delayed don't necessarily mean miracles denied? What is the "something better" (v. 40) that God has provided for us?

Optional Activities

1. Break into groups of two or more and share an experience of when God divinely invaded your life to help you through a difficult circumstance. Brainstorm specific ways you can reach out to help others who are praying for a miracle involving the same circumstances you've already faced. Perhaps you are God's answer to their prayers!

2. Reflect on the author's statement: "Suffering has a way of sharpening our perspective—of clarifying and bringing into focus what is good and what is bad, what is necessary and what is superfluous, what is holy and what is unholy." In what ways have your experiences with suffering in this life clarified your focus on what is truly important?

Prayer Focus

Thank God for His promise that He is working everything out for your good and His glory. Ask Him to help you "set your mind on the things above" (Col. 3:2), and then transform your suffering into praise as you look forward to heaven!

Assignment

1. This week, be careful not to let your desire for a miracle come between you and Jesus. Remember: The object of your faith is Christ, not miracles.

2. Read chapter 7 of *Divine Invasions* and work through the corresponding study.

CHAPTER 7

BEWARE OF COUNTERFEIT MIRACLES

Session Topic

The Bible is clear that "our struggle is not against flesh and blood, but against the rulers, against the powers, against the world forces of this darkness, against the spiritual forces of wickedness in the heavenly places" where Satan rules (Eph. 6:12). To avoid falling for deceptive "signs and wonders" (2 Thess. 2:9), we must first understand how the father of lies operates.

Icebreakers (Choose One)

1. Have you ever believed something or someone to be genuine, only to realize later that you'd been scammed? Describe what happened.

2. What are some ways we can prevent ourselves from being scammed? How can we learn to recognize and avoid a scammer?

Group Discovery Questions

1. Satan is portrayed in Scripture as extremely powerful and influential. Read John 12:31, 2 Corinthians 4:4, and Ephesians 2:2, and discuss what you learn about Satan.

2. Though the devil's power is great, it's not as great as God's power. Discuss what you learned in this chapter about God's characteristics of being *omniscient*, *omnipresent*, and *omnipotent*. (Look up these words in a dictionary if needed.) In what ways do these aspects of God differ from Satan's power? Why is that significant?

3. Read Exodus 7:8–13, 20–22, and 8:5–7, and discuss what you learn about counterfeit miracles. According to these verses, who gave Moses and Aaron the power to do miracles? Who do you think empowered Pharaoh's magicians to do counterfeit miracles? Do you think these miracles looked similar or different? Explain your answer.

4. Discuss the author's statement: "Beware of counterfeit miracles. Just because something looks impressive and inexplicable doesn't automatically mean it's divine; it could be demonic." Based on your reading this week, how do we determine whether a miracle is divine or demonic?

5. What does the author refer to as "the gold standard for all truth"? Discuss the dangers of relying on our experiences, feelings, or the beliefs of a friend or relative to determine if a miracle is real or counterfeit.

6. Read Acts 17:10–12. In this passage, how did the Bereans respond to Paul's preaching? What can we learn from the Bereans' example as we are confronted with various teachings today?

7. Consider the author's statement: "False teachers don't necessarily tip their hand so easily by denying Christ outright. Rather, they masquerade their lies as truth by failing to affirm Christ clearly." Discuss some ways false teachers today undermine God's Word stealthily and with a smile. Give specific examples, if possible. What can believers do to avoid being scammed by counterfeit miracles and false teachers?

Personal Application Questions

1. In many churches today, Satan's power is often downplayed, as if he were practically harmless. Look up the following Scriptures and write what the Bible teaches about Satan's power here on earth: For Satan's power over *humans*, see Luke 13:11, 16; Acts 10:38; 16:16; for *governments*, see Matthew 4:8–9; 2 Corinthians 4:4; for *angels*, see Ephesians 6:11–12; Jude 9; and for *religion*, see Revelation 2:9; 3:9.

2. According to the author, "False teachers typically concentrate their attacks by using three counterfeit messages. First, *false teachers don't confess Jesus as Christ—the Anointed One*." Read 1 John 4:2 and write how this verse equips us to discern whether a teacher is genuinely from God.

3. "Here's the second counterfeit message of false teachers: *False teachers don't confess Jesus as coming in the flesh—the incarnation.*" Read 1 Corinthians 15:18–19 and write what this passage teaches about the importance of the incarnation and bodily resurrection of Jesus Christ.

4. "Failing to confess Jesus as both Christ and as having come in the flesh leads to the third message espoused by false teachers: *False teachers don't confess Jesus as Lord—the sovereign God.*" Read 1 Corinthians 12:3 and write what you learn from this verse about how to determine whether someone's message is genuinely from the Lord or a counterfeit from Satan.

5. Read Matthew 7:15–16. According to Jesus, how can we recognize a false teacher? What did Jesus mean by "their fruits"? See Matthew 12:33–36 for more insight on this.

6. When evaluating those who claim to be miracle workers or miracle recipients, we must beware of counterfeit motives. What did you learn in your reading about the motivations of ungodly teachers? How can we tell if a preacher is motivated by personal gain rather than the people's good?

7. Consider the author's warning: "Make no mistake, false teachers usually possess a charismatic personality. But don't confuse charisma with character." In your own words, what's the difference between *charisma* and *character*? Why is it important for believers to focus on a teacher's character when evaluating his or her message or miracles?

Optional Activities

1. Make a list of unbelievers you know in your family, workplace, school, and community. Ask God to give you opportunities to talk with them, and commit to sharing the gospel of salvation with them.

2. Accepting God's invitation to eternal life is the only means for a divine invasion—the greatest miracle of all: your salvation. If you would like to become a Christian and know for sure that one day you will be welcomed into heaven, you are invited to pray this prayer, knowing that God is listening:

   Dear God,

   Thank You for loving me. I realize I have failed You in so many ways. And I am truly sorry for the sin in my life. I believe You love me so much that You sent Your Son, Jesus, to die on the cross for me, to take the punishment I deserve for my sin. And right now, I am trusting in what Jesus did for me—not in my good works—to save me from my sins. Thank You for forgiving me. Help me to spend the rest of my life serving You. In Jesus's name, amen.

Prayer Focus

Thank God for the many insights and challenges He has brought to you through this study. Ask Him to help you continue to grow in your understanding of His miracle-working power and to experience a deeper sense of awe for how He is divinely invading your life today, as well as how He will continue to divinely invade your life in the future.

ABOUT DR. ROBERT JEFFRESS

Dr. Robert Jeffress is senior pastor of the sixteen-thousand-member First Baptist Church, Dallas, Texas. Located in the heart of downtown, First Baptist Dallas is built on the Bible and has been reaching the city, nation, and world for Jesus Christ for more than 150 years. Led by Dr. Jeffress since 2007, the church completed a $130 million renovation and expansion in 2013 and now occupies six city blocks—enhancing the church's ability to carry out its mission of transforming the world with God's Word . . . one life at a time.

Dr. Jeffress is a FOX News contributor and appears regularly on FOX News Channel's *FOX & Friends*, *FOX News @ Night*, *Hannity*, and *The Faulkner Focus* and on the FOX Business Network. Dr. Jeffress has made more than four thousand guest appearances on television programs that include HBO's *Real Time with Bill Maher* and Trinity Broadcasting Network's *Praise*.

Established in 1996, *Pathway to Victory* serves as the broadcast ministry of Dr. Jeffress and exists to pierce the darkness with the light of God's Word through the most effective media available. The daily radio programs air on over a thousand stations, and in 2025 the National Religious Broadcasters Association recognized *Pathway to Victory* with its prestigious Radio Program of the Year award. The daily television program can be seen on over eleven thousand cable and satellite systems, including Trinity Broadcasting Network (TBN), where it has been the number one most-watched program since 2020. *Pathway to Victory* broadcasts are translated into six languages and reach 193 countries throughout the world in addition to all major markets in the USA. On each daily broadcast, Dr. Jeffress provides practical application of God's Word to everyday life through clear, uncompromised biblical teaching. Additionally, *Pathway to Victory* ministers globally through podcasting, social media, and other digital media.

Dr. Jeffress is the author of more than forty books, including *Not All Roads Lead to Heaven*, *A Place Called Heaven*, *Choosing the Extraordinary Life*, *Courageous*, *Invincible*, *18 Minutes with Jesus*, *What Every Christian Should Know*, *The 10*, and *Jesus Revealed in the End Times*.

Dr. Jeffress graduated with a DMin from Southwestern Baptist Theological Seminary, a ThM from Dallas Theological Seminary, and a BS from Baylor University. He was awarded a Doctor of Divinity degree from Dallas Baptist University and received the Distinguished Alumnus of the Year award from Southwestern Baptist Theological Seminary. He is also an adjunct professor at Dallas Theological Seminary.

Dr. Jeffress and his wife, Amy, have two daughters and three grandchildren.

ABOUT *PATHWAY TO VICTORY*

Established in 1996, *Pathway to Victory* serves as the broadcast ministry of Dr. Robert Jeffress. *Pathway to Victory* stands for truth and exists to pierce the darkness with the light of God's Word through the most effective media available, including television, radio, print, and digital media.

Through *Pathway to Victory*, Dr. Jeffress spreads the good news of Jesus Christ to a lost and hurting people, confronts an ungodly culture with God's truth, and equips the saints to apply Scripture to their everyday lives. More than a thousand radio stations in the United States broadcast the daily radio program, which was awarded the 2025 Radio Program of the Year by the National Religious Broadcasters Association. TBN, Daystar, and other television networks and stations air *Pathway to Victory* in the United States and internationally.

Our mission is to provide practical application of God's Word to everyday life through clear, biblical teaching. Our goal is to lead people to become obedient and reproducing disciples of Jesus Christ, as He commanded in Matthew 28:18–20. As our ministry continues to grow and expand, we are confident the Lord will use *Pathway to Victory* to transform the world with God's Word . . . one life at a time.